BEFORE AND DURING READING ACTIVITIES

Before Reading: *Building Background Knowledge and Vocabulary*

Building background knowledge can help children process new information and build upon what they already know. Before reading a book, it is important to tap into what children already know about the topic. This will help them develop their vocabulary and increase their reading comprehension.

Questions and Activities to Build Background Knowledge:

1. Look at the front cover of the book and read the title. What do you think this book will be about?
2. What do you already know about this topic?
3. Take a book walk and skim the pages. Look at the table of contents, photographs, captions, and bold words. Did these text features give you any information or predictions about what you will read in this book?

Vocabulary: *Vocabulary Is Key to Reading Comprehension*

Use the following directions to prompt a conversation about each word.

- Read the vocabulary words.
- What comes to mind when you see each word?
- What do you think each word means?

Vocabulary Words:

- activists
- discrimination
- documentaries
- funding
- Parliament
- protested
- rights
- segregates

During Reading: *Reading for Meaning and Understanding*

To achieve deep comprehension of a book, children are encouraged to use close reading strategies. During reading, it is important to have children stop and make connections. These connections result in deeper analysis and understanding of a book.

 Close Reading a Text

During reading, have children stop and talk about the following:

- Any confusing parts
- Any unknown words
- Text to text, text to self, text to world connections
- The main idea in each chapter or heading

Encourage children to use context clues to determine the meaning of any unknown words. These strategies will help children learn to analyze the text more thoroughly as they read.

When you are finished reading this book, turn to the next-to-last page for **Text-Dependent Questions** and an **Extension Activity**.

Table of Contents

Who Has a Right to Education?

Who has a right to education? You do! A group of countries called the United Nations made rules about the **rights** of children around the world. The rules said, "Everyone has the right to education."

This rule had to be made because not all kids can get an education. Millions of children around the world do not go to school. Kids face different problems that get in the way. These include child marriage, having to work, and **discrimination**.

Kids in Noida, a city in India, attend a local school. Small schools can make a big difference.

Adults sometimes force children to marry. This is called child marriage. It is not fair to children. Eleven-year-old Payal Jangid's parents wanted her to get married. She asked for help from local **activists**. Once she was safe, she started working for children's rights. Payal went door to door in her village in India. She talked to children and parents. She spoke out against child marriage. She explained the importance of going to school.

Payal continued to speak out. She became the leader of the Child **Parliament** in her village. Adults and children listened to her. Payal wants to become a teacher in the school in her village someday.

A Visit with the Obamas

In 2015, Payal Jangid was invited to meet President Barack Obama and the First Lady when they visited India. Payal said she felt like "the luckiest girl in India."

Girls in School

In most of the world, the number of young boys and girls in school is equal. But in some places, more girls are out of school than boys. Some of these places are Sub-Saharan Africa, the Middle East, and South Asia. In these places, many girls work all day instead of going to school.

Education Is Important

Education affects people's lives. People with more education earn more money on average. They often have more choices and opportunities.

Ten-year-old American Zuriel Oduwole has been called the world's youngest filmmaker. Both of her parents' families are from Africa. She visited Africa to make many of her **documentaries**. She saw a lot of poor girls. They were working. They were not in school.

Zuriel started Dream Up, Speak Up, Stand Up to help girls get an education. She talked to thousands of girls. She has talked with presidents and prime ministers about the importance of education and girls in school.

Zuriel Oduwole, once called "The World's Most Powerful Girl" was honored at the Women In Film Awards.

The Taliban is a group of people that doesn't think women and girls should have an education. The Taliban took over Malala Yousafzai's town in the country of Pakistan when she was 10. She loved her school. She knew the Taliban could make it against the law for her to go to school.

But Malala wanted to go to school. She wanted all girls to go to school. She knew that if she spoke out, she might be harmed. But, she said, "In hard times, we need to raise up our voice."

Malala Yousafzai

"ONE CHILD, ONE TEACHER, ONE BOOK, AND ONE PEN CAN CHANGE THE WORLD."
– Malala Yousafzai

Malala **protested** school closings. She gave her first speech at age 11. She wrote news stories. She went on TV. Finally, girls in her area were allowed to go back to school if they covered their heads.

Malala faced threats for saying what she believed. She was the victim of an attack. Malala was in the hospital a long time. But Malala never quit speaking out. She said, "I determined to continue my fight until every girl could go to school."

Malala gives a speech about the importance of education at the United Nations.

NON-FICTION BOOK OF THE YEAR

WINNER
OF THE
NOBEL
PEACE
PRIZE

I Am *Malala*

I Am Malala

Malala Yousafzai wrote a book, *I Am Malala*, when she was 1
years old. She is the youngest person to ever receive the No
Peace Prize.

Not All Schools Are Equal

The public school you go to is based on your school district. People draw lines on maps to make school districts. Sometimes, the lines make it so that some schools have more money than others. Poorer neighborhoods can have poorer schools. This **segregates**, or separates, the rich from the poor.

Schools in richer neighborhoods might have bright classrooms, lots of books, computers, and art supplies. Many schools in poorer neighborhoods do not. Sometimes, the lines also make it so that some schools are segregated by race.

Nine-year-old Asean Johnson learned that 54 schools in Chicago, Illinois, were about to be closed. His school was on the list. Asean did not want to lose his school. So, the fourth grader spoke out at a rally to hundreds of people.

Asean spoke out and said most of the schools on the list were schools in African American communities. He even called on the mayor to save the schools. The city still closed schools. But they didn't close Asean's school.

Asean Johnson speaks to a crowd about the importance of his school.

Asean didn't give up. He wanted to keep speaking out about equal education rights. He went to the *Realize the Dream* rally. It was on the 50th anniversary of the March on Washington in Washington, DC. This march was where Martin Luther King Jr. gave his famous *I Have A Dream* speech.

Asean spoke at the rally. He said that all schools should have equal **funding**. He talked to a huge crowd. He stood up "for education, justice, and freedom."

Just like Payal, Zuriel, Malala, and Asean, you can speak out! Join these advocates and help change the world!

Realize the Dream march and rally

Realize the Dream

At nine years old, Asean was the youngest person to ever speak at the Realize the Dream rally.

Top 10 Ways to Get Involved

 1 Spread awareness about inequality in education by wearing a shirt or a button with a message.

 2 Write a letter to a leader in your community or nation to ask for change.

 3 Start a club for change and invite other students to join you.

 4 Research how other communities have made changes. Try an idea in your community.

 **5** Attend a peaceful rally with an adult to learn more about the issues.

 6 Create brochures that explain the importance of education. Pass them out.

 7 Hold a book drive. Send the books to children around the world who don't have books.

 8 Create a poster about the importance of education. Post it where people can see it.

 9 Join a peaceful march to ask for change you care about.

 10 Ask your teacher to start a global pen-pal club. Learn about education around the world.

Glossary

activists (AK-ti-vists): people who work to make political or social change

discrimination (dis-krim-i-NAY-shuhn): unfair behavior to another because of age, race, gender, etc.

documentaries (dahk-yuh-MEN-tur-eez): movies or television programs about real people and events

funding (FUHN-ding): money provided for a specific purpose

Parliament (PAHR-luh-muhnt): a group of people who make the laws in some countries

protested (pruh-TEST-ed): spoke out loudly and publicly

rights (rites): things you are legally or morally entitled to have

segregates (SEG-ri-gates): separates or keeps people or things apart

Index

Text-Dependent Questions

1. Who has the right to an education?
2. How many children do not go to school around the world?
3. Name one benefit that comes from getting an education.
4. Name three things children can do to speak out for education.
5. What do Payal, Zuriel, Malala, and Asean have in common?

Extension Activity

Think about your experience at school. What is your favorite subject? Are there any computers? Do you like your teacher? Are there any after-school clubs or teams you like? Make a list of things you are grateful for about your school experience. Find out about schools that do not have these things. Decide what to do to help.

About the Author

Chris Schwab is a writer and editor. She has written many articles for newspapers and magazines. She also used to be a teacher and knows the value of an education. Now she writes books for kids. She loved learning from the awesome kids who spoke out about education!

Quote sources: "The Universal Declaration of Human Rights," United Nations, 1943: https://www.un.org/en/universal-declaration-human-rights/; Taniya Dutta, "The 'luckiest girl in India': Meet the children's rights activist, 14, who hugged Michelle Obama and was praised for her work – but still refused the First Lady's gift," Daily Mail, January 30, 2015: https://www.dailymail.co.uk/news/article-2933400/The-luckiest-girl-India-Meet-children-s-rights-activist-14-hugged-Michelle-Obama-praised-work-refused-gift.html;
Malala Yousafzai, "16th birthday speech at the United Nations," Malala Fund, July 12, 2013: https://www.malala.org/newsroom/archive/malala-un-speech; PBS NewsHour, "Malala explains why she risked death to speak up for girls' education," PBS, September 16, 2014: https://www.pbs.org/newshour/show/malala-explains-risked-death-speak-girls-education; "Malala's story," Malala Fund, 2018: https://www.malala.org/malalas-story; Fred Klonsky, "Asean Johnson, Chicago 9-Year-Old, Youngest Speaker At March On Washington Anniversary," Huffpost, August 26, 2013: https://www.huffpost.com/entry/asean-johnson-march-on-washington_n_3817494

www.rourkeeducationalmedia.com

PHOTO CREDIT: Cover, p1 ©ronniechua, ©Nikada, ©calvindexter, ©Hulinska_©Yevhenila, ©Bubushonok; p4 ©epicurean; p5 ©AbhishekMittal; p6 ©Andrew Babble; p7 ©Jim Bourg; p8 ©By Somchai_Stock; p9 ©FatCamera; p10 ©AB1; p11 ©Yury Birukov; p12 ©khlongwangchao; p13 ©JStone; p14 ©TMP - An Instant of Time; p15 ©SN040288; p16 ©Cynthia Farmer; p17 ©slobo, ©Tonktiti; p18 ©bjphotographs; p19 ©Anthony Souffle; p20 ©Joseph Sohm.

Edited by: Hailey Scragg
Cover and interior layout by: Kathy Walsh and Morgan Burnside

Library of Congress PCN Data

Kids Speak Out About Education / Chris Schwab
(Kids Speak Out)
ISBN 978-1-73163-859-5 (hard cover)(alk. paper)
ISBN 978-1-73163-936-3 (soft cover)
ISBN 978-1-73164-013-0 (e-Book)
ISBN 978-1-73164-090-1 (ePub)
Library of Congress Control Number: 2020930057

Rourke Educational Media
Printed in the United States of America
01-1942011937